W9-DIO-441

★
ICONS

Cover:
Oldsmobile, 1957

Endpapers:
Oldsmobile, 1952

© 2002 TASCHEN GmbH
Hohenzollernring 53, D–50672 Köln
www.taschen.com

Editor: Jim Heimann
Design: Sense/Net, Andy Disl & Birgit Reber, Cologne
Cover Design: Andy Disl, Claudia Frey, Cologne
Production: Tina Ciborowius, Cologne

Printed in Italy
ISBN 3–8228–1630–2

50ˢ CARS

Jim Heimann

TASCHEN

KÖLN LONDON MADRID NEW YORK PARIS TOKYO

Lincoln, 1950

Lincoln, 1950

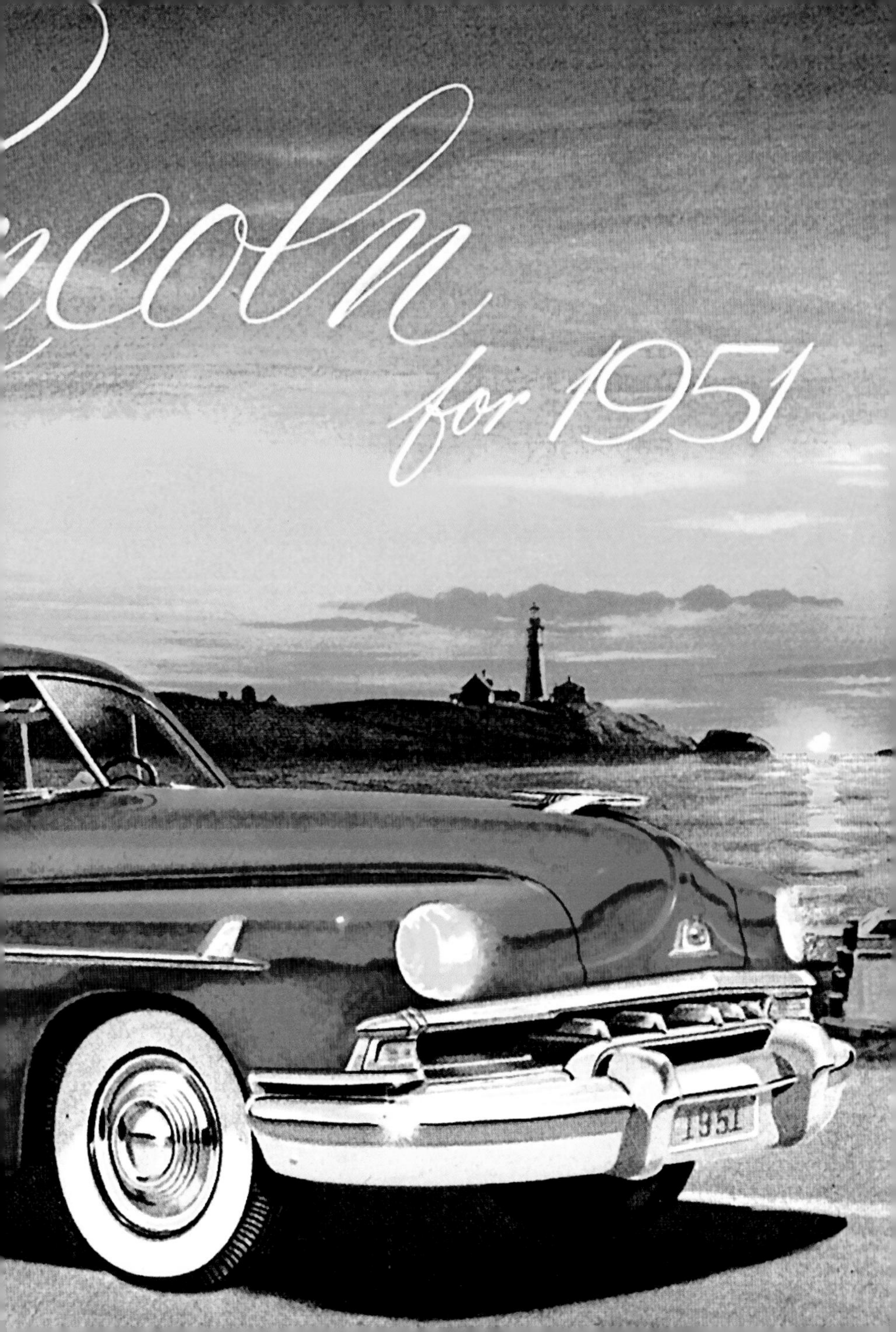
ncoln
for 1951
1951

Pontiac, 1951

▲*Lincoln, 1952*

▼*Nash, 1950*

▲Henry J, 1950

▼Mercury, 1950

▲*Pontiac, 1951*

▼*Mercury, 1951*

Mercury, 1952

Stretch Out and See

NEW SPACE-PLANNED DESIGN— No unused space—this is the new lean-back-and-take-it-easy Mercur that puts every inch of car to work And looks? "Forerunner" styling i years ahead.

Why It Challenges Them All

Standard equipment, accessories and trim illustrated are subject to change without notic. White side-wall tires, when available, at extra co

NEW SEA-TINT* GLASS reduces heat, glare, and eyestrain. New larger windows permit safety-sure visibility all around. *Every view* proves that Mercury is new—in looks, in power, in extra value.

WE BUILT A NEW CAR and made this challenge: Match Mercury *if you can.* Now we know we've got the sweetest thing on wheels since the ladies began to drive.

For all America is falling in love with a car.

No wonder. It's big and beautiful, inside, outside, and all over. With a host of Future Features—Forerunner styling, Jet-scoop hood, suspension-mounted brake pedal, Interceptor instrument panel, higher horsepower V-8 engine—the new Mercury is the most challenging car that ever came down the *American Road.*

See it, drive it. You'll fall in love, too. And with Mercury's famous economy—*proved* in official tests— this is a love affair you can afford.

MERCURY DIVISION · FORD MOTOR COMPANY

The New 1952

MERCURY

WITH MERC-O-MATIC DRIVE

3-WAY CHOICE—Mercury presents three dependable, performance proved drives: silent-ease, standard transmission; thrifty Touch-C Matic Overdrive,* and Merc-O-Matic,* greatest of all automatic drive

*Optional at extra co

Ford, 1951

Cuts 92% of your driving motions! New Fordomatic Drive* does your gear shifting for you. It's America's newest, finest, most flexible automatic transmission!

*Optional at extra cost.

Stretch your driving dollars—with Ford's Automatic Mileage Maker! You get high-compression performance with regular gasoline! A new Waterproof Ignition System prevents engine "shorts" from moisture.

No car is better finished, better built! There's quality that lasts in the quiet elegance of Ford's new Luxury Lounge Interior, in the soundness of Ford's coachwork!

All the best

FOR THE YEARS AHEAD

Enjoy "Fashion-Car" styling—from the new recessed headlights to new Jet-Styled Windsplits. Ford's designed to stay "right" in the years ahead!

Feel the safety of an extra-heavy steel Luxury Lifeguard Body! And Ford's new Double-Seal King-Size Brakes keep out dirt and water—give smooth, safe stops in any weather!

"Test Drive" the '51 Ford . . . at your Ford Dealer's today. And as you drive it, remember that this car is built for the years ahead! With 43 "Look Ahead" features, it was planned and engineered to stay young in performance, to stay in style, to stay thrifty —for years to come!

YOU CAN PAY MORE
BUT YOU CAN'T BUY BETTER!

Relax with Ford's new Automatic Ride Control! It adjusts your ride to any road *automatically!* The going stays easy, level— no pitch, no jounce, no roll!

'51 Ford

PAINTED FOR PLYMOUTH BY NORMAN

"Merry Christmas, Grandma... we came in our new PLYMOUTH!"

Plymouth, 1950

Help yourself to the open road and as far as the eye can see in *any* direction! Ford's new Victoria gives you the "wide-openness" of a convertible and the comfort of a trim sedan!

Ford, 1951

Take your pick of a wide variety smart solid or two-tone body colo And the Victoria's "Luxury Loung Interior features long-weari Craftcord-leather-vinyl upholste combinations, luxurious modern tri and a new "Safety-Glow" Contr Panel—all keyed to outside colors

You've got the world by the wheel in the

'51 FORD VICTORIA!

Relax as you ride! Ford's Automatic Ri Control smooths out the bumps before the can reach you. The Automatic Posture Co trol front seat insures the most comfortab driving position. What's more, you have th assurance of Ford's Luxury Lifeguard Bod with a solid steel top, and Ford's double-dre box-section frame with five cross member

You're set for the years ahead—with 43 "Look Ahead" features from Key-Turn Starting to extra-big "Tell-Tale" Rear Lights and "Double-Seal" King-Size Brakes! See the '51 Ford Victoria—"Test Drive" it—today at your Ford Dealer's.

You get power to match the "let's go" look of the Ford Victoria—the famous 100-h.p. V-8 engine and your pick of Conventional Drive, Overdrive* or the new Fordomatic Drive*. With any of them, Ford's Automatic Mileage Maker delivers high-compression performance on regular gasoline!

You can pay more but you can't buy better!

*Overdrive, Fordomatic Drive and white sidewall tires (if available) optional at extra Equipment, accessories and trim subject to change without notice.

NOW—a fine car that meets every test of modern living

Lincoln for 1952

IN TWO INCOMPARABLE SERIES—

THE Cosmopolitan —THE Capri

NEW GLASS-WALL VISIBILITY—There's a new way of life in America—reflected in today's glass walled rooms for modern living. Lincoln, too, surrounds you with glass—3271 square inches. With chair-high seats and down-sweep hood, even the daintiest woman driver can see the right front fender—see the road in front and way ahead. Every line has a reason.

Standard equipment, accessories, and trim illustrated are subject to change without notice. White-wall tires, when available, optional at extra cost.

NEW FLIGHT-LIKE POWER—There's ready-to-fly excitement in Lincoln's completely new, overhead-valve, high-compression, V-8 engine—premium product of the company that has built more V-8's than all other makers combined. With HYDRA-MATIC Transmission (as standard equipment), and new ball-joint front suspension (first on a standard U.S. car), steering and handling are astonishingly effortless.

NEW VERSATILE SMARTNESS—This is beauty with purpose. Right for trip or town, a business car, a family car—with more leg room, more head room, almost 30 cu. ft. in the luggage compartment. Yet Lincoln is smartly sized to thread through traffic, park easily, fit your garage. *The one fine car deliberately designed for modern living.*

LINCOLN DIVISION—FORD MOTOR COMPANY

Lincoln, 1952

SMART YET CASUAL—LIKE THE MODERN HOSTESS. Clean-lined, without gingerbread, the new Lincoln is proof that a fine car can be as handsomely functional as the new-day homes—and new-day living. Inside, you find superb fittings—and the seats are high, the hood is low; you can *see* the road directly ahead, you can *see* the world all around through 3,721 square inches of glass (sea-tint glass available).

VERSATILE AS A LIVING ROOM DESIGNED FOR LIVING. Lincoln is luxurious yet maneuverable, beautiful yet *powerful.* New V-8 engine, with overhead valves, 7.5 to 1 compression ratio—plus new, improved dual range HYDRA-MATIC Transmission. And, with new ball-joint front wheel suspension, first on a U.S. production car, handling becomes astonishingly easy.

Standard equipment, accessories, and trim illustrated are subject to change without notice. White-wall tires optional at extra cost.

IN TWO INCOMPARABLE SERIES— THE COSMOPOLITAN—THE CAPRI

Now⎯ LINCOLN

makes your driving as modern as your living

It is completely new. It is almost incredibly new. But more than this—it is an entirely new *approach* to fine automobiles, designed for those whose concept of luxury motoring does not include the common, the ponderous, or the unwieldy.

Lincoln for 1952 is for those who ask their car to match their new perspective on living. Though it may well be the most luxurious automobile on the *American Road*, it is magnificently *functional.*

There is a reason for every dimension. There is a purpose behind each line. The new Lincoln is spirited, compact, and surpassingly efficient.

There is only one way to know this new kind of motoring—this fine car that is like a feather in traffic, an arrow on the road. That way is to try it and to drive it. See the new Lincoln Cosmopolitan and Capri at your dealer's showroom. Lincoln—*the one fine car deliberately designed for modern living.*
LINCOLN DIVISION—FORD MOTOR COMPANY

Lincoln, 1952

Lincoln, 1952

Lincoln, 1952

These keys unlock GREATER VALUE.

HERE are the five new cars General Motors offers you for '52.

Each has a famous name of its own: Chevrolet, Pontiac, Oldsmobile, Buick, Cadillac.

Each has its own personality in styling, appointments, features, power.

But all enjoy an advantage which stems from the research into better ways to do things—the testing of everything from the integrity of metal to the soundness of design — the broad knowledge of engineering and manufacturing methods which General Motors provides.

The results, as you will discover, are comfort, convenience, performance unknown a few years ago.

Each year witnesses new advances—and we believe you will find these newest cars, now readied for the market, the finest we have built thus far.

We invite you to see them now at your local GM dealer's — and you will know why "your key to greater value" appears on the key of every car.

"MORE AND BETTER THINGS FOR MORE PEOPLE"

GENERAL MOTORS

General Motors, 1952

OR YOU IN '52!

Hear HENRY J. TAYLOR on the air every Monday evening
over the ABC Network, coast to coast.

— Your Key to Greater Value — The Key to a General Motors Car —

27

NINETY-EIGHT HOLIDAY SPORTSEDAN

Every 1959 Oldsmobile has the smart new "Linear Look"—trim, light, wide-open, spacious! Inside and out it's aglow with bright ideas—safer brakes, improved visibility, smoother ride, more luggage room. Yes, and a brand-new Rocket Engine, too! An engine that is incredibly smooth, the most efficient Rocket yet. Think a moment. Isn't it time to step up to an Olds—*acknowledged leader in the medium price class!* Talk it over with your local quality dealer.

OLDSMOBILE DIVISION,
GENERAL MOTORS CORPORATION

OLDSMOBILE FOR '59

Oldsmobile, 1959

Pontiac creates an entirely new type of car

combining Catalina smartness

and station wagon utility

This completely new Star Chief from the originator of hardtop styling is easily the most versatile of motor cars. Appointed with traditional Catalina luxury, yet retaining all the spacious practicality of a station wagon, the Safari will serve you equally well as a smart town car, a wondrously comfortable touring companion, or a hard-working carrier. It is powered, of course, by the sensational Strato-Streak V-8 for performance as distinctive as its beauty. See it today—the price will delight you as much as the car!

THE PONTIAC

Pontiac, 1955

Hand-buffed leather in coral and ivory, deep-pile matching carpet and color-keyed instrument panel and wheel typify the luxurious new interiors of the '54 Custom Catalinas.

Dollar for Dollar You Can't Beat a

PONTIAC

A GENERAL MOTORS
MASTERPIECE

America's First Low Cost Luxury Car

You are looking at the new wonder of the motoring world, the completely new Star Chief Pontiac. And what makes this car such a wonder is its unsurpassed combination of superb quality and low price. *There has never been anything like it.* For here is the biggest, richest and most powerful Pontiac ever built—qualified by length, luxury, styling and performance to rank with the very finest cars. Yet the proud and beautiful Star Chief can adorn your driveway no matter how carefully you budget new car expenditures. It is still comfortably within the price range just above the lowest!

And America's first low cost luxury car is only half the great news from Pontiac. For 1954, the Chieftain, General Motors lowest priced eight, is also mightier than ever and far more beautiful inside and out—again the dominant dollar for dollar value at its very modest cost.

Check Pontiac's remarkable score for '54. See, drive and price these distinguished new Silver Streak Pontiacs. Prove to your pleasure and profit that never before have quality and low cost been so beautifully combined.

You compress time....distance

- in effortless ease
with the first
complete driver control

You cannot pass unnoticed in a stunning
car like this. Exuberant new color and bold
sweep of line draw the eye like a magnet.
But flattering and thrilling, too, is your new
power over time and distance. PowerFlite, most
automatic of all no-clutch transmissions,
multiplies your safety with control of motion that's
entirely new. The 235 HP FirePower V-8 engine gives
you instant power for instant response at all times. Power Steering
is easy and safe as pointing. Power Brakes halt you swiftly and surely with
but ⅓ the pedal pressure of conventional brakes. All these combine in
the first complete driver control. A new day in driving ease and safety. A new
day that is yours to enjoy just as soon as you visit your nearby Chrysler dealer.

and look

The Power of Leadership is yours in a **BEAUTIFUL CHRYSLER**

31

Plymouth, 1956

Buick Roadmaster, 1953

Ford, 1953

Pontiac, 1955

Pontiac, 1955

Buick Roadmaster, 1955

Buick Roadmaster, 1954

Buick Roadmaster, 1954

Buick, 1956

▲Cadillac, 1955

▲*Chevrolet, 1955*

▼Buick, 1954

▲ Cadillac, 1956

▼Pontiac, 1958

▲Chrysler, 1952

▼ *Buick, 1953*

With Flying Colors...

1955 Oldsmobile Super "88" Holiday Coupé. A General Motors Value.

OLDSMOBILE 88

ROCKETS INTO 1955 !

Oldsmobile, 1955

NEW!

NEW!

ALL-AROUND-NEW!

Flashing into the future with flying colors . . . *Oldsmobile for '55!* . . . *more spectacular, more colorful, more powerful* than ever! In three exciting series (Ninety-Eight, Super "88", "88"), every one of them new, all-around-new, *all the way through!* And Oldsmobile's owner-proved "Rocket"—the engine that blazed the way into the Power Era—is all-new, too! New 202 horsepower, new higher torque, new higher compression ratio—new combustion chambers! Every new Oldsmobile has that commanding new "Go-Ahead" look—bold, sweeping front-end design—dramatic new "flying color" patterns—dazzling new styling from front to rear—the newest *new ideas on wheels!* More than ever, Oldsmobile is out ahead to *stay ahead!* See your dealer now . . . see these magnificent new "Rocket" Oldsmobiles for 1955!

Pontiac, 1954

Cadillac, 1955

Thunderbird

Chevrolet, 1957

▲Chevrolet, 1956

▼Mercury, 1955 (cf. pp. 48/49)

Pontiac, 1956

Star Chief Four-door Catalina

Oldsmobile, 1959

Avis Rent-A-Car & Ford, 1958

USA-1958

AMERICA'S NO.1 ROAD CAR

SURF CLUB

Cadillac, 1956

The car conceived and created
to change your ideas of luxury motoring

This is sweeping line and commanding length. This is unusual richness of interior cushioning and appointment. This is uncompromising precision. This is the LIMITED. It is the car we conceived and created to outmode the present measure of fine cars. It is the car you will drive with a new sense of magnificence that grows out of its performance, its comfort, its excellence of construction. Your Buick dealer cordially invites you to see the distinguished LIMITED—and to take a personal demonstration behind its wheel. See him for an appointment.

PROUDLY PRESENTED, PROUDLY POSSESSED *The*

LIMITED

by Buick GM 1908·1958

We deliberately designed it

Beyond a doubt, this newest of fine cars goes well beyond the familiar concepts of luxury and performance. Indeed, that was our goal in creating the LIMITED. Thus, its interior presents a degree of elegance and comfort that sets a new level of magnificence. Its performance exceeds existing standards — to the point of providing a wholly new experience in ease of handling and serenity of ride. Even in the matter of its extra length, the LIMITED goes beyond the call of familiar dimensions. You will find this superbly crafted automobile a most satisfying possession — and your Buick dealer will be understandably proud to introduce you to it.

BUICK *Division of* GENERAL MOTORS

be the world's finest automobile

PROUDLY PRESENTED, PROUDLY POSSESSED — *The*

LIMITED

by Buick

GENERAL MOTORS
GOLDEN MILESTONE

Cadillac, 1956

The Sixty Special

Cadillac for 1957... brilliantly

ew in beauty, brilliantly new in performance!

The Eldorado Biarrit

Cadillac Eldorado

This is the Eldorado—a new adventure in automotive design and engineering—with brilliant and dramatic styling . . . hand-crafted, imported leather interiors . . . "disappearing" top . . . and a sensational 270-h.p. engine. In all that it is, and does, and represents . . . it is the finest fruit of Cadillac's never-ending crusade to build greater quality into the American motor car.

Now in limited production • Price on request

Eldorado

BY CADILLAC

CADILLAC MOTOR CAR DIVISION • GENERAL MOTORS CORPORATION

Cadillac, 1956

Cadillac presents

the greatest advancements it has ever achieved

in motor car styling and engineering !

▲Buick Roadmaster, 1957

▼Buick

▲*Chrysler, 1958*

▼*Oldsmobile, 1952*

▲*Oldsmobile, 1959*

▼Thunderbird, 1958

Imperial, 1957

Oldsmobile, 1951

De Soto, 1956

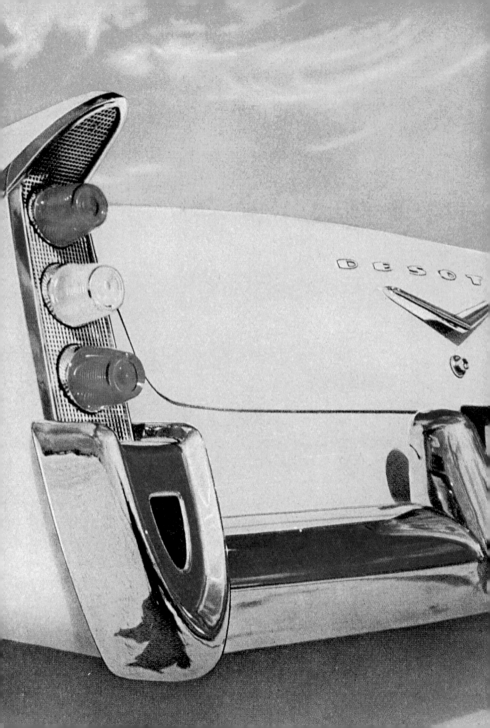

Buick, 1959

Ford, 1957

'58 CHEVROLET

The 1958 Chevrolet Impala in Anniversary Gold, a new color created in commemoration of General Motors 50th Anniversary Year.

The biggest, boldest move any car ever made! *For more about it, turn the page...*

THE CAR: BUICK '59

ELECTRA 225 IN THE EYE-STOPPING NEW 4-DOOR HARDTOP

LE SABRE
The thriftiest Buick

INVICTA
The most spirited Buick

ELECTRA
The most luxurious Buick

Here it is...and now you know! Know why we have called this THE CAR. Know that a new generation of great Buicks is truly here. From just this one view you can see that here is not just new design...but a splendidly right design for this day and age. A car that is lean and clean and stunningly low...and at the same time great in legroom and easy to get into and out of. From anywhere you look, here is a classic modern concept that is Buick speaking a new language of today. A language of fine cars priced within reach of almost everyone. A language of quality and comfort and quiet pride...a language of performance satisfactions without equal.

New Bodies by Fisher • New Easy Power Steering* • New Twin-Turbine and Triple-Turbine automatic transmissions* • New Wildcat Engines • New Equipoise Ride New, improved, exclusive aluminum front brake drums and fin-cooled rear brakes
*OPTIONAL AT EXTRA COST ON CERTAIN MODELS.

A NEW CLASS OF FINE CARS WITHIN REACH OF 2 OUT OF 3 NEW CAR BUYERS

▲ Buick, 1959

▼ Chevrolet, 1957

New luxury and distinction—the Bel Air Impala Sport Coupe.

Almost too new to be true!

'58 CHEVROLET

Here's styling that sets a new style! The beautiful '58 Chevrolet is nine inches longer, four inches wider and up to 2½ inches lower.

The bold new Bel Air 4-Door Sedan.

CHEVROLET

From dual headlights to gull-wing rear fenders, these are truly impressive cars. Interiors, wheelbases, grilles, styling accents, fabrics and appointments—everything is new, luxurious, exciting!

The stylish new Nomad Station Wagon.

Never, never has a car been so wonderfully new in so many different ways! Here are radical departures in style, power and ride...all wrapped up in the longest, lowest, widest Chevrolet that ever said, "C'mon, let's get going!"

Here are just *some* of the real surprises that await you in Chevrolet's three new series, its new line of station wagons, its eye-brightening array of 17 all-new models:

A revolutionary new V8! So new it even looks different on the outside—that's Chevy's Turbo-Thrust V8*! Combustion chambers are in the block—a radical design development that results in super-smooth performance and high efficiency. Horsepower ranges up to 280. There are three new versions of the famous Turbo-Fire V8, too, including Ramjet Fuel Injection*, and more power for the super-thrifty Blue-Flame Six.

New body-frame construction! The secret of Chevy's road-hugging lowness is the new X-design Safety-Girder frame. There's extra safety in the lower center of gravity...and new locked-together strength in the way this new frame is welded to Chevrolet's new Body by Fisher.

All-new 4-coil suspension! Here's a fabulous combination of super-soft coil springs *and* the super stability of Chevy's exclusive four-link rear suspension. Unquestionably, the finest standard suspension in Chevrolet's field!

You can even ride on air! Level Air suspension* puts air springs at every wheel for the ultimate in thistledown comfort. It changes every contour of motoring smoothness—and the car stays level, regardless of load changes front or rear!... See the year's newest car at your Chevrolet dealer's... Chevrolet Division of General Motors, Detroit 2, Michigan.
*Extra-cost option

YOUR EYES. YOUR HEART. YO

T

BUICK

E GOOD SENSE TELL YOU IT'S...

HE CAR

59

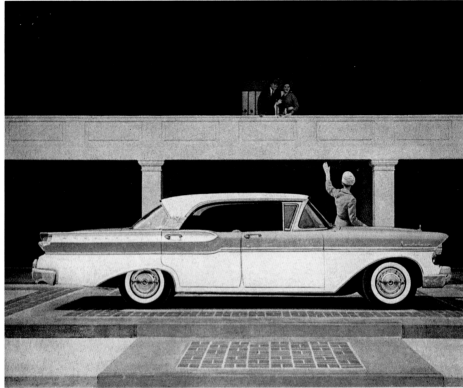

THE MERCURY MONTCLAIR PHAETON SEDAN

Beauty shared by no other car—biggest size and value increase in the industry

EXCLUSIVE DREAM-CAR DESIGN. Here is clean-lined beauty, a massive grace, that is Mercury's alone. Notice the distinctive Jet-Flo bumpers, V-angle tail-lights.

FAMILY-CAR BIG

There's stretch-out comfort for six. This year's Mercury is bigger in 8 vital dimensions inside, 4 outside. There are inches of spare head-room, hip room, shoulder room, and leg room.

PRICED FOR EASY BUYING

Never before has so much bigness and luxury cost so little. See for yourself. Ask your BIG M dealer for the fun-to-read figures, today.

ONLY MERCURY OFFERS YOU THESE 6 DREAM-CAR FEATURES

- Exclusive Dream-Car Design
- Exclusive Floating Ride, with 4 new bump-smothering features
- Exclusive Power-Booster Fan in Montclair Series
- New Merc-O-Matic Keyboard Control
- Power seat that "remembers".
- New Thermo-Matic Carburetor

THE BIG MERCURY for '57 *with DREAM-CAR DESIGN*

MERCURY DIVISION • FORD MOTOR COMPANY

Just born—and bound to make history!

the first big car that's light on its feet—

YOU LOOK at it—and you see "BIG" written all over this bold and beautiful 1958 Buick.

You drive it—and you know that never in all your born days have you known a car so nimble, so eager, so light on its feet.

It took plenty to bring you this easiest-handling, sweetest-riding Buick ever built.

It took a brilliant new engine—the B-12000 —which packs 12,000 pounds of punch behind every piston's power stroke.

It took a brilliantly engineered transmission —Flight Pitch Dynaflow*—that swings its blades through infinite angles of pitch to give precise response to every ounce of pedal pressure.

It took the wonders of the 1958 Buick Miracle Ride—plus the perfection of Buick Air-Poise Suspension*—and Buick Air-Cooled Aluminum Brakes*—and a combination of other modern advances you'll find nowhere but in a 1958 Buick.

But surely you can't be content just to sit there and *read* about all these wonders! Hurry in to your Buick dealer's and *see* and *feel* what he has in store for you!

BUICK *Division of* GENERAL MOTORS

Flight Pitch Dynaflow standard on LIMITED and ROADMASTER 75, optional at extra cost on other Series. Air-Poise Suspension optional at extra cost on all Series. Aluminum Brakes standard on all Series except SPECIAL.

Big·Bold·Buoyant
the AIR BORN B-58 BUICK

Buick, 1957

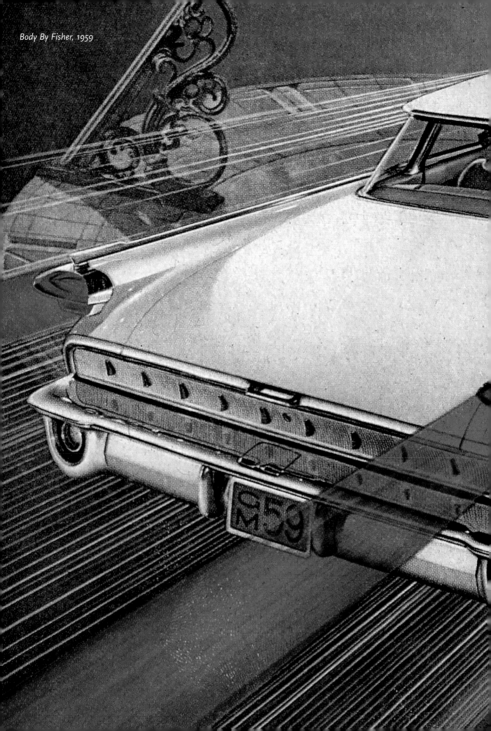
Body By Fisher, 1959

Oldsmobile, 1958

Pontiac Bonneville, 1958

Motoring's Action-packed Aristocrat . . . Connoisseurs of cars invariably note the unique quality that distinguishes Pontiac's Bonneville from all other fine car breeds. Here, perfectly wedded with an indelible luxury and elegance, is the exhilarating dash and verve of a true high-performance road car! To see and drive the Bonneville, whether the superb Sport Coupe or its equally illustrious teammate, the Convertible, is an un-forgettable experience. Why not try it?

BOLD
NEW Bonneville  BY PONTIAC

You get the solid quality of Body by Fisher.

Gorgeous new way to save as you go!

Pontiac's new V-8, the Tempest 420E, gives you phenomenal extra mileage—up to 20% saving on gasoline bills!

The same engineers who developed the new Tempest 420 V-8 to give you the ultimate in *action* have also developed a companion power plant with unbelievable gasoline economy! This new engine is a big, easy-breathing V-8 . . . yet it uses *regular gas* and delivers

better mileage than many of the smaller cars with so-called "economy engines"! Result? *You save up to 20% on gasoline bills!* The secret is in its amazingly efficient design . . . perfected by the industry's hottest engineering team to give you the extra gas mileage you want *without sacrificing V-8 rim and vigor!* So if you have the idea that economy and action just can't go together you're in for a wonderful surprise!

PONTIAC MOTOR DIVISION · GENERAL MOTORS CORPORATION

EXCLUSIVELY YOURS—*WIDE-TRACK* WHEELS

The widest, steadiest stance in America—better cooling for engine and brakes, better grip on the road, safer cornering, smoother ride, easier handling. *You get the most beautiful roadability you've ever known—in America's Number ① Road Car!*

PONTIAC! America's Number ① Road Car!

3 Totally New Series · Catalina · Star Chief · Bonneville

See Victor Borge on Pontiac Star Parade, Nov. 29—CBS-TV

121

This is the # EDSEL

"A remarkable new automobile   joins the Ford family of fine cars"

Originally as written in the vertical grille, the elegant sweeping lines and the clean flight deck of this Edsel Citation 2-door Hardtop

There has never been a car like the Edsel. It is a magnificent automobile. Behind it lie all the resources of Ford Motor Company, all the experience and engineering skill.

The results are clear. The Edsel is powered by the newest V-8 engines in the world—the Edsel 400 and the Edsel 475. Their specifications: 400 and 475 pound-feet of torque; 303 and 345 horsepower; 361 and 410 cubic inches of displacement; 10.5 to 1 compression ratio. It is unlikely you have ever driven a car with so much usable power. The Edsel's big, safe brakes do not need periodic adjustment. In the course of daily driving, they adjust automatically.

The Edsel shifts itself. In an Edsel equipped with Teletouch Drive, you just touch a button on the steering wheel hub. Teletouch Drive does the rest—smoothly, surely, safely, electrically.

The Edsel's list of available new features is long. Examples: contour seats; a dial that lets you select temperature, quantity and direction of air with one twist of the wrist; a warning signal that flashes when you exceed your pre-set speed limit; another that flashes when oil is one quart low; a release that enables you to open the luggage compartment from the driver's seat. You will find there are many things that make the Edsel different from any car you have ever driven. More exciting, more sure, more safe.

What does an Edsel cost? Edsel prices range from just above the lowest to just below the highest. You can afford an Edsel. And you can choose from four series, 18 models. Your Edsel Dealer invites you to see and drive the Edsel—soon.

EDSEL DIVISION · FORD MOTOR COMPANY

EDSEL
NOW AT YOUR EDSEL DEALER

▲ *Edsel, 1951*   ▼ *Thunderbird, 1958*   ▶ *Diamond Chemicals*

Ford presents a brilliant   new version of a great classic...the 4-passenger

T H U N D E R B I R D

America's most individual car—an automotive jewel that's pure Thunderbird in design, spirit and performance...with full fine-car room, comfort and luxury for four

Another first from Ford! In the 1958 Thunderbird, Ford has created a wholly new size and type of fine car. It gives you Thunderbird compactness, Thunderbird handling and traditional Thunderbird performance— yet, miraculously, it now gives you full fine-car room and comfort for four people! It brings you interior appointments that are unbelievably imaginative and luxurious. Now, happily, you can share your Thunderbird thrills with deserving friends. Now it's *twice the fun* to own the car that became an American classic the very day it was introduced. For details about America's most excitingly different car,

turn the page, please

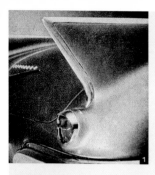

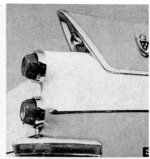

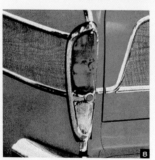

Diamond's Guide to Car Watching
(can you identify them?)*

Here are the southern exposures of nine northbound 57's. Dramatically different as these new cars are, they have one thing in common. On each is some chrome plating that started with DIAMOND Chromic Acid. DIAMOND ALKALI is one of the world's largest producers of chromium chemicals, and DIAMOND research has recently developed a new additive for chrome platers which reduces plating time and cost, gives a harder, brighter finish.

Progress like this helps explain why DIAMOND's "Chemicals you live by" are preferred by so many industries, found in so many places.
DIAMOND ALKALI COMPANY, Cleveland 14, Ohio.

Diamond Chemicals

* 1. CADILLAC   2. CHEVROLET   3. DODGE   4. FORD   5. MERCURY   6. OLDSMOBILE   7. PLYMOUTH   8. RAMBLER   9. STUDEBAKER

Chevrolet, 1958

Oldsmobile, 1959

Cadillac, 1956

HOTEL
AMBASSADOR
EAST

22724

De Soto, 1957

Pontiac Bonneville, 1958

Pontiac, 1958

USA-1958
AMERICA'S NO.1 ROAD CAR

Pontiac, 1958

Lincoln, 1959

Classic elegance in motorcars: The Lincoln Landau. Gown by Traina-Norell

THE CLASSIC FINE CAR

that brings Continental luxury within the reach
of every fine car buyer

THE NEW LINCOLN

styled and crafted in the classic Continental tradition

Inspiration for The New Lincoln: the new Continental Mark III.
Mark III prices are just slightly above the fine car field.

The New Lincoln—styled and crafted in the Continental tradition—has created a new standard by which all fine cars must now be measured.

For the first time, every fine car owner has the opportunity to know Continental standards of luxury, driving qualities and craftsmanship.

The man who owns a Lincoln drives a car of classic beauty. And as he drives, he knows the pleasure of being surrounded by classic elegance in interiors.

The Lincoln owner knows an engine built to a whole new standard of precision tolerances . . . and in the Continental ideal of luxurious, *effortless* driving—every power assist known.

We invite your inspection of the first distinctively new choice in fine cars in many, many years.

LINCOLN DIVISION, FORD MOTOR COMPANY

Now, in America, a refreshing new concept in fine motor cars

The excitement it stirs in your heart when you see the Continental *Mark II* lies in the way it has dared to depart from the conventional, the obvious.

And that's as we intended it. For in designing and building this distinguished motor car, we were thinking, especially, of those who admire the beauty of honest, simple lines . . . and of those who most appreciate a car which has been so conscientiously crafted.

The man who owns a Continental *Mark II* will possess a motor car that is truly distinctive and will *keep* its distinction for years to come.

Continental
Mark II

Continental Division · Ford Motor Company

Chevrolet, 1959

▲Buick

▼Oldsmobile, 1959

A GENERAL MOTORS VALUE.

OLDSMOBILE'S

FABULOUS NEW

"*Starfire*"

NOW IN PRODUCTION!

Starfire—the "show car" that can be your car! *Starfire*—with a long, rakish, waist-high silhouette . . . smartly curving panoramic windshield and spectacular sweep-cut rear fenders . . . saddle-stitched leather interior in dramatic new two-tone patterns. *Starfire*—with the surging might of a new 185-horsepower "Rocket" Engine! See and drive this glamorous new Oldsmobile convertible—the "Dream Car" Ninety-Eight *Starfire*—at your Oldsmobile dealer's now.

"Be careful—drive safely!"

Johnny and Lucille, Oldsmobile's singing sweethearts, invite you to ride the "Rocket" . . . to drive Oldsmobile's sensational new Super "88"!

TRY 160 H.P.

"ROCKET" ACTION

...in the New Super "88"

You've got to drive it to believe it! Never before has Oldsmobile had such an exciting performance story to tell! For here is a *new* kind of "Rocket" Engine car—*dramatically new* with the flashing 160-h.p. "Rocket" . . . now paired with smooth new Hydra-Matic Super Drive*! The result is performance that truly *stands out* even in this era of high-powered motor cars! GM Hydraulic Steering*, the Autronic-Eye*, and many other new features add to your motoring comfort and safety. Drive Oldsmobile's Super "88" . . . you'll never settle for anything else!

Hydra-Matic Super Drive, GM Hydraulic Steering, Autronic-Eye— and white sidewall tires (when available) optional at extra cost. Equipment, accessories and trim, subject to change without notice.

A General Motors Value

"ROCKET" POWERED OLDSMOBILE

147

Ford, 1958

Cadillac, 1958

THE FLEETWOOD SIXTY SPECIAL

A NEW

THE 1959 *Cadillac*

By appointment to the world's most discriminating motorist.

THE ELDORADO BIARRITZ

EALM OF MOTORING MAJESTY!

ngle glance tells you these are the newest and most mag-cent Cadillac cars ever created. Dazzling in their beauty, ee and elegance, and inspiring in their Fleetwood luxury decor—they introduce a new realm of motoring majesty. l a single journey at the wheel will reveal still another fact nat these are the finest performing Cadillacs ever produced. h a spectacular new engine, more responsive Hydra-Matic

drive and improved qualities of ride and handling, they provide a totally new sense of mastery over time and distance. This brilliant new Cadillac beauty and performance are offered in thirteen individual body styles. To inspect and to drive any of them is to acknowledge Cadillac a new measure of supremacy. We invite you to do both—soon! CADILLAC MOTOR CAR DIVISION • GENERAL MOTORS CORPORATION

THE SIXTY-TWO COUPE

Oldsmobile, 1959

Pontiac, 1959

Mercury, 1959

Oldsmobile, 1957

Rambler, 1959

33
pu
eng
rati
spe
by

...wer Performance from a 550-Pound Motor — GM engineers solved the problem of
...ry high-powered engine in small space by developing an entirely new light alloy
...oth of these cars. The engine is a supercharged V-8 having 10 to 1 compression
...perating on premium-grade fuel for all normal driving — premium fuel plus
...suitable for supercharged engines at higher speeds. Engines are supercharged
...GM engineers developed for Diesel engines.

Once around with J-WA

ans **and** waxes your car!

Mobilgas, 1953

Mobilgas, 1950

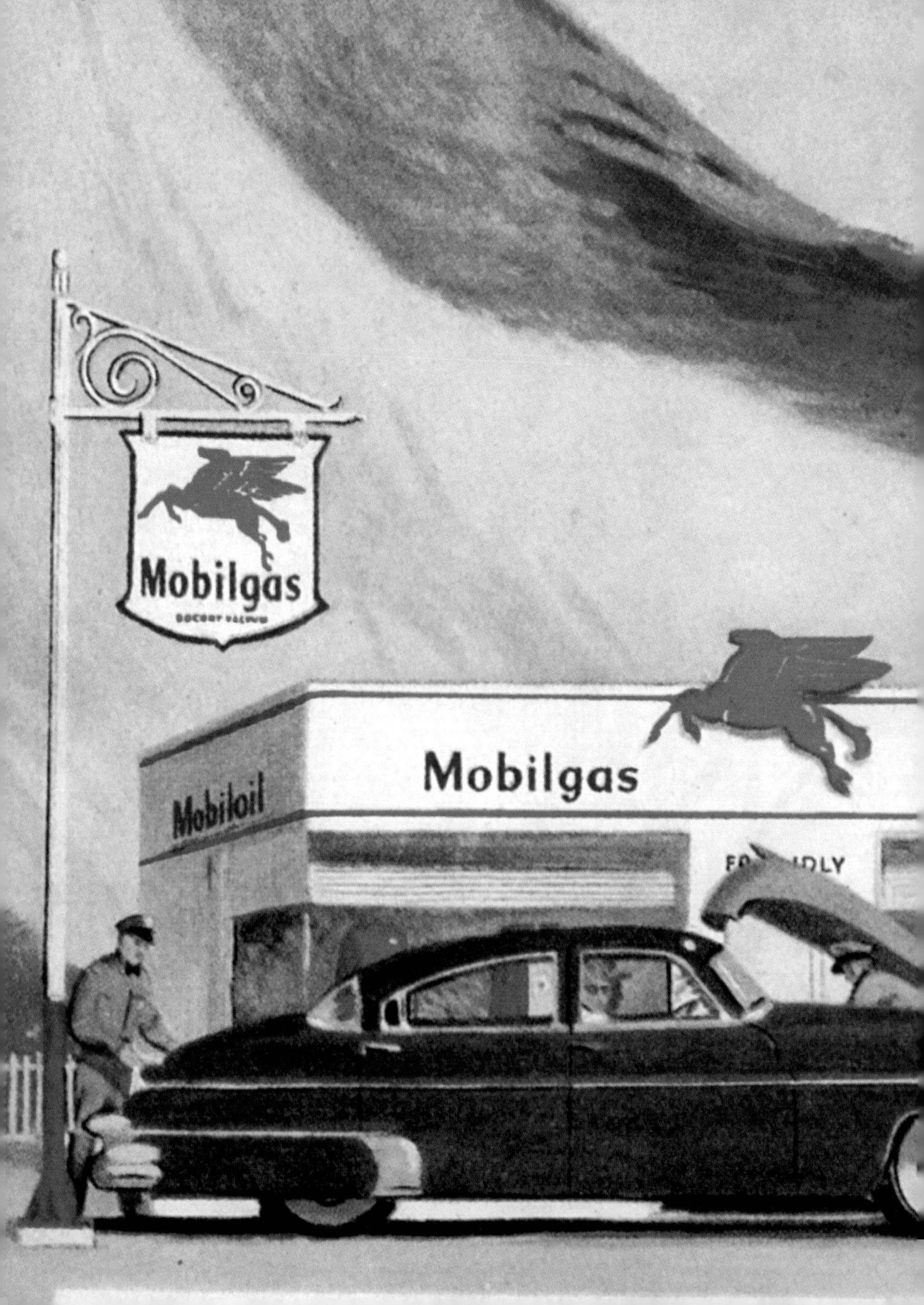

AC Spark Plugs, 1957

Gulf Oil

Shell Motor Oil, 1951

Your engine makes this much Acid every day

... And it's Acid Action—not friction—
that causes 90% of engine wear

New Alkaline Shell X-100 Motor Oil counteracts Acid Action

If you are a typical motorist, in a normal day's driving:—a pint or more of acid is formed and passes through your car's engine, and it's acid action, not friction, that causes 90% of your engine wear. To neutralize the harmful effect of this acid, Shell Research has produced an alkaline motor oil—Shell X-100. Fortified with alkaline "X" safety factors, it neutralizes the acid action, prolonging the life of your engine.

The new Shell X-100 is a Premium Motor Oil. It is a Heavy Duty Motor Oil. In addition, it contains positive cleansing factors that help protect hydraulic valve lifters and other vital parts from fouling deposits.

Shell X-100 is the finest motor oil money can buy. Let your Shell dealer give your engine the protection of this new alkaline Shell X-100 Motor Oil today.

It's Incomparable!

SHELL X-100 MOTOR OIL PREMIUM-HEAVY DUTY

FOR YOUR WINTER OIL... CHANGE TO

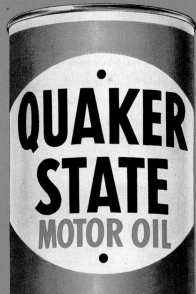

QUAKER STATE MOTOR OIL

Whether *your* winter driving is through ice and snow or in southern sunshine—Quaker State Motor Oil is tailor-made for *your* car. Skillfully refined from 100% Pure Pennsylvania Grade Crude Oil, Quaker State is the product of continuous research, engine-testing and 50 years of specialization in automotive lubrication. It gives your car complete lubrication and long-lasting protection.

QUAKER STATE OIL REFINING CORPORATION, OIL CITY, PA.
Member Pennsylvania Grade Crude Oil Association

Quaker State Motor Oil, 1953

Sinclair, 1959

introducing...

rom Sinclair's Space-Age Research

NEW 3-STAGE GASOLINE

OVER 100-OCTANE NO INCREASE IN PRICE

New Sinclair Power-X Gives You 100-Octane Performance in All 3 Driving Stages

1 **STARTING** Power-primed with rocket fuel, new Power-X Gasoline is over 100-octane! You start quick as a click in any weather...and your engine warms up smooth and sweet. No stalling, no skipping.

2 **ACCELERATION** 12,000 pounds thrust at the touch of your toe! No need for fancy super-priced gasolines. With new Power-X, you get lightning getaway...reserve power for smoother, safer driving.

3 **MILEAGE** Those extra octanes mean extra economy, too...more miles in every thrifty gallon. And there's no increase in price! Watch for the new Power-X at your neighborhood Sinclair Dealer's Station.

NO PRICE INCREASE

SINCLAIR
POWER-X
OVER 100 OCTANE

SINCLAIR

WATCH FOR THE ARRIVAL OF NEW POWER-X GASOLINE IN YOUR COMMUNITY

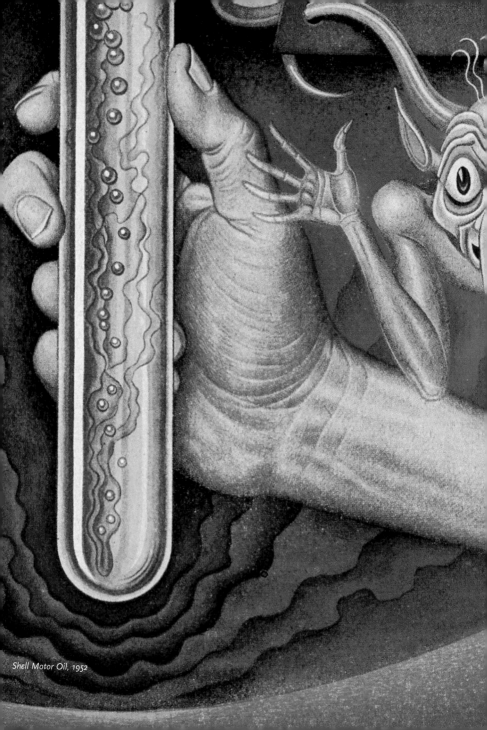

Shell Motor Oil, 1952

WASHING   GULFLEX

Gulf Oil, 1957

Edsel, 1958

ICONS

"Buy them all and add some pleasure to your life."

www.taschen.com

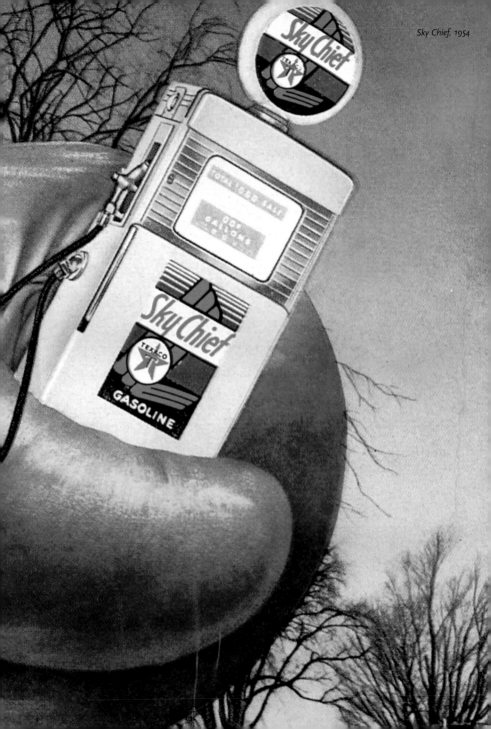

Sky Chief, 1954